For Brautigan Zeus

Copyright ©2018 by Jessica Laurel Kane

All rights reserved. No part of this book may be reproduced, transmitted, or stored in an information retrieval system in any form or by any means, graphic, electronic, or mechanical, including photocopying, taping, and recording, without prior written permission from the publisher.

First edition 2018

Library of Congress Catalog Card Number: 2018911751
ISBN 978-1-7328682-0-5

Printed in China

This book was typeset in JollyGood Proper.
The illustrations were created using paper cut-outs, edited digitally.

Visit the author at www.jessicalaurelkane.com

YMMSBILYA PRESS

FEED IT TO THE WORMS

a collection of very short stories for small children

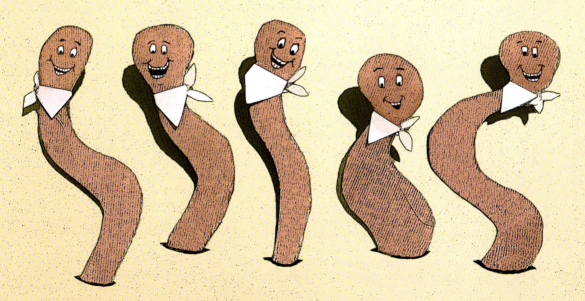

written and illustrated by Jessica Laurel Kane

My Elevator

Here's a secret: I have an elevator in my body. Yup. And it takes me wherever I want to go.

I press the button for the top floor to get good ideas.
I press the heart button when I want to feel love.
When I forget who I am, I press my center button.
And when I forget where I am, I always press the ground floor.

But sometimes, I let other people press my buttons and this causes a lot of mayhem. Especially when other people press that one red button that sends me flying through my own roof.

It's scary out there. Especially when I'm yelling for that same person to send me back to where I wanna be and they've already gone and can't even hear me!

But the thing I'm realizing more and more about all this, is that other people aren't even in my elevator. As far as I can tell, I'm the only one here. Which means other people can't really press my buttons. Only I can. So I guess the trick is remembering to take myself where I want to go, instead of where I don't.

The Boy Who Befored His Daddy's Ear

Once upon a time, a little boy befored his daddy's ear. If you don't know what it means to before something, it means to remove it and send it back to Mother Nature to the time it existed before it was born.

The little boy didn't know exactly what he was doing because he just learned this magic. And so the daddy lost his ear until a year later, when it got born again, which was a problem because the ear was really, really small like a newborn's, but it was on the head of the daddy that was still daddy-sized. And all the people said, "Whoa, that daddy sure has a tiny ear!"

The daddy tried to make it work, but this was hard sometimes, because from that tiny ear, he couldn't understand words. He heard like a baby. So he laughed a lot when people spoke to him on that side because they sounded so funny. But thankfully, most people understood what had happened and were ok with it. They just spoke to his bigger ear.

And by the time enough years went by, his tiny ear grew up and everyone lived happilier ever after.

The End.

The Unanswerable Question

Mommy, do you love me?
Yes, baby.
Do you love me more than you've ever loved anyone?
Yes, baby.
Do you love me now?
Yes.
What about now?
Yes.
Do you love me more than you loved me yesterday?
Yes, baby.
But... what was wrong with me yesterday?

The Kind King

    So there was this dragon and he was trying to break into my castle to steal my treasure. So naturally, I stuck him in my dungeon and he started crying. Not like my other prisoners, though. This dragon kept crying and saying the words, "My dog!!! *My dog!!*"
    "What about your dog," I finally yelled down.
    "Who's gonna feed my dog?"
    "Dragons have pets?"
    He nodded yes and kept on and on with the crying and the drooling so finally I said, "Ok ok, give me your address and I'll fetch your gosh-forsaken dog."
    So I took my horse and buggy to Dragon Avenue to the last house on the block and sure enough, when I finally managed to open the giant green door, I see this tiny regular-sized dog crying his eyes out. So I bundled him up and brought him back to the castle and stuck him down in the dungeon with the dragon and they must have hugged each other for three thousand hours. And every night since, I lower two bowls of food down there. And they seem much happier.

The End.

Too Many Toys

Did you hear the one about the boy with too many toys? Whose family kept giving him more and more toys and then yelling at him to pick them all up when he never brought them to the house to begin with?

The boy whose mom and dad said *enough is enough* and went on a cleaning strike even though the boy's aunts and uncles and all their aunts and uncles still sent boxes of toys that blocked the front door so the family couldn't even get out of the house?

Well, that boy is me! So if any kids want a lot of toys please come get them so I can go to school!

Thank you!

Mean Red

My name is Redmond but everyone calls me Mean Red because I'm mean. I heard a couple people whispering about me the other day. They were wondering why I'm so mean. And it got me thinking. I've known for a while that I'm good at being mean because I make a lot of kids cry. But I never really thought about how I got this way. So I thought about it and remembered.

See, I wasn't always mean. I used to be real friendly. But then something happened: One afternoon, my mom took me to a playground. And while she was on her phone, I introduced myself to these four kids and asked if they wanted to be my friends. But they told me I wasn't big enough to be their friend.

I tried to show them that I was a big kid. I even showed them my best somersault, but they laughed at me, and then one of them told me their brother could do the same thing when he was one. So I said ok, and I showed them how I could do the monkey bars. But I was so nervous, I fell down. And when I started to cry, they laughed at me again and walked away together leaving me on the ground all by myself.

And it was at that moment, I decided never to be nice to anyone again. And I came up with this idea, that I would be the mean one first. That way, no one would ever get the chance to be mean to me, 'cause I'd beat them to it. And it worked. No one's been mean to me since. But that was two years ago. And I still don't have any friends. And I wish I did have a friend. Someone to be nice to. Someone who might want to build a tunnel with me at the sandbox sometime.

So if you're reading this, and you see me all alone on the playground, don't be afraid. Now you know I was only mean because I was afraid you wouldn't want to be my friend. So if you still want to be my friend, just let me know. And I promise I'll be a good one.

The End.

The Girl With Seven Ears

This is a story about a girl I know who has seven ears.
That's right.
She can hear the fish in the pond from three towns away.
She can hear the ice machine in the refrigerator down the street.
She can even hear the thoughts of her teacher.
But you know what's funny?
I heard she doesn't listen to her mother.
Especially when her mother tells her it's time to clean her ears.

The End.

The Three-Legged Cow

So this little girl had this toy cow at the playground. And there was this little boy there who really wanted it. The cow only had three legs and he'd never seen anything like it. And he couldn't stop staring at it. And then the little girl left it on the pirate ship by the steering wheel and the little boy found it. He told himself it was a finder's keeper and tried to forget that he knew full well whose it was. And he put it in his pocket and went on the tire swing and felt great. Really, great. Until he heard someone crying. It was the girl. She was crying to her mama and he really hoped it was 'cause she fell and skinned her knee. But it wasn't. She was crying because she lost her favorite toy.

And the little boy wished he hadn't heard what she was saying. But he did hear. That this three-legged cow had belonged to her great grandfather. And that he'd played with it when he was her age. And that his son had played with it. And his son. And so on and so on. Basically, he found out that this toy had survived like a hundred years without any damage other than its missing leg.

And he tried again to convince himself that it was no big deal but this cow was burning up in his pocket. And then his mama said, "Honey, your face is bright red, are you ok?" And the boy started crying and told the whole story. "Well, you know what you have to do," she said.

He begged his mama to do his dirty work, but they both knew it was his job. So he sighed and his mama gave him a kiss on his head and he walked over to the little girl. And when he handed her the cow, she gave him the biggest hug. And that's when he decided he didn't need to tell her the whole story. He knew what happened. And that's what counts.

And he never took anything that wasn't his ever again. Well, except when it was a real finder's keeper.

The End.

Thinking Cap

I feel like hitting and punching.
Why?
I don't know.
Is your thinking cap on?
My thinking cap?
Come on. You don't know what a thinking cap is?
Nope.
It's built into your brain.
How do you get it to work?
You just ask it to work.
How?
Well, if you're feeling scared, you dial it to brave. If you're being reckless, you dial it to wise. If you're hurting someone's feelings, you dial it to kind.
What if you're hungry...?
If you're *hungry?!!* Then you get up and go make yourself a sandwich!!!

The Day Everyone's Feelings Got Hurt

Once there was a little boy who asked a little girl if she wanted to play, but the little girl said, "*No,*" and the little boy's feelings got hurt. A few minutes later, another little boy asked him to play, but because his feelings were still hurt, he didn't even hear the question, and so this other little boy got upset and yelled, "Well, *fine* then. I don't want to play with you *either!*"

A little while later, another little girl asked the angry little boy to play, but all he could say was, "*Go away,*" because *his* feelings were still hurt, and the little girl started to cry.

Then another girl walked over to comfort her, but she was so afraid this new girl was going to be mean that she cried for her mommy, and this new girl got upset.

Then, a little boy asked *this* upset little girl if she wanted to play and she thought about it and said, "*No,*" because she was afraid she might have misunderstood the question. And so on and so forth until every little boy and every little girl in the whole wide world was upset.

Eventually, a new little girl arrived at the playground and noticed a sad little boy all alone. The little girl asked if he wanted to play, but the boy shook his head no, because his feelings had just been hurt by someone else. But instead of getting upset, this little girl decided to do something different. She asked him a question. "Is there something wrong?" she asked the boy. "Are you upset? You look upset." And the little boy nodded yes. And so she asked, "Do you need a friend?" And the little boy nodded yes again. And so they played and played until some other boys and girls asked if they could play too. And they said, "Yes, of course you can!"

And pretty soon every boy and every girl in the whole wide world were playing together again.

The End.

The Big Misunderstanding

A penguin and a lion were waiting for the bus one day. The lion was going on and on about how sad he was. How he was tired of doing the same old thing day in and day out. The penguin was trying to help him. "You've got to appreciate what you have, Lion, instead of focusing on all the things you don't." And then, out of nowhere, the lion and the penguin were surrounded by official-looking people who assumed incorrectly that they'd escaped from the zoo. And the penguin and the lion were kidnapped.

They tried to explain to their captors that they had never ever lived in a zoo. That they had an apartment together and made their living selling crafts online. But the people didn't believe them. And the zookeeper stripped them of their clothes and belongings and put them in a cage right next to the elephants and rhinos.

The lion was really depressed now and the penguin said, "Well, I suppose this is going to be the moment you're gonna start begging for your old life?" And the lion said, "*Please*, now is not the time to get on my last nerve." And the penguin rolled his eyes and picked the lock with his beak and the lion and the penguin left the zoo and took the bus naked back to their apartment. But at the door, they realized they didn't have their keys. And the lion was all ready to bash it down when the penguin turned the knob. "Oh," said the lion. "I guess we forgot to lock it."

Inside, the lion leaned back on the couch and smiled while the penguin drank tea. "Well, Penguin," he said. "I guess there really is no place like home."

The End.

The Boy Who Was Afraid To Cry

      Once there was a boy who got really upset, but he couldn't figure out a good time to cry. And then, he forgot he even had to cry. His tears knew, though. And they kept trying to get out. Even when the boy was happy, these tears would try to get out. And the boy was always nervous.
      He didn't want to listen to sad music. Or when people said they loved him. In fact, it was only when he was mean that he wouldn't get the feeling like he had to cry. And so people started leaving him alone. Which got him upset all over again.
      Before long, he had so many tears stuck inside, that he could hardly get around. And then there was a geyser.
      Out of nowhere, just walking through the grocery store, it burst out of his eyes and even out of his mouth and ears.
      And all the people who saw, stopped and watched as everything he was sad about finally leaked all over the place: the time his mom and dad yelled at each other, the time his grandma got sent back to heaven, the time his favorite toy broke, the time nobody wanted him on their team... on and on. And everyone was so sad with the boy, they all started crying together.
      They cried and they cried until all of their tears nearly flooded the world.
      And then, all they had left was peace.
      And all they had to figure out was what to do next...

The Little Boy And His Friend

Once there was a little boy who had a little friend that looked exactly like him. And one day, they were in their room together and the one boy said, "I think I smell smoke," and the other boy agreed. Luckily, they knew what to do. They called 911 and waited outside for the helpers to arrive.

A minute later, a very loud fire truck whizzed into the driveway and as the fire fighters unfurled their hoses, one of them asked the boy if there was anyone else in the house. And that's when the boy realized he'd left the other boy inside.

He cried when he realized this, and the firefighter gave him a hug and said, "It's ok. We'll get him right away!" And she carried the little boy back into the house so he could lead her to his friend. And the boy took her into his bedroom, to the mirror on the wall, and when they were standing in front of it, he cried, "There he is! Right there!"

And so she took the mirror off the wall and carried them both to safety. And as the little boy hugged his friend, the firefighter told him he was a hero. And then she told his mama to make sure not to forget about the oatmeal in the pot ever again.

The End.

The Girl Who Wouldn't Take A Bath

Once upon a time there was a girl who wouldn't take a bath. Even her mother had to wear a clothespin over her nose to get close enough for a hug.

"*Please!*" her mother begged. "Please take a bath!!!"

But she wouldn't.

In time, the smell got worse. People knew she was coming from a mile away.

Then parsnips began to grow on her arms. And mushrooms on her legs. And soon she couldn't wear shoes 'cause of the carrots on her feet. Finally she cried, "Ok, Mama, I'm ready! I'm ready for my bath!!!"

But it was too late.

They had to hire a farmer, who drove to their house in his combine harvester. And though the vegetables came off easily, the dirt was still so thick.

"How 'bout we hose her down," her father asked.

"*Go ahead, Daddy,*" the little girl cried.

Finally her mother saw a gleam, a sliver of flesh! "My *baby!!!*" And she ran to her muddy daughter and hugged her up tight.

And after the last of all the mud came off, the little girl finally took her bath. And another one every night thereafter.

The End.

Ripping Service

Once there was a boy who had a ripping service. His job was to rip apart everything that could rip. Whenever his mommy got upset with him about this, he simply explained: "Mama, I have to rip. I have a ripping service."

He ripped receipts and bags and boxes and itineraries and taxes and photographs, but his favorite thing to rip by far were library books.

His mother became especially stern about the library books. "*This is where I draw the line,*" she scolded. "If you don't tape all these pages back together right now, I'll be forced to cancel all playdates until further notice!"

"Ok, Mama," the boy said. "But I'll have to call Joe down the street first, to see if his taping service is still in business."

And then the boy sang to his mama his favorite song: "Da da da da da da... da!"

The Reluctant Rescuer

There was a boy who climbed up a really giant haystack, but while he was getting to the top, a volcano erupted and a piece of the volcano landed on the haystack and it caught on fire. The boy was so scared he called 911. Rescuer Brautigan Zeus answered with a yawn, "What's your emergency?" The boy explained his situation in a panic, "Please, can you help me? The fire is getting closer!"

Brautigan yawned again, "I'm not sure. I *was* sleeping."

"You were sleeping? But..." The boy started crying, in even more of a panic, "I thought you were a rescuer! You're Brautigan Zeus, right?"

"Yes, yes."

"But the fire is getting closer!"

"Fine, fine. I'll come."

"Will you be driving your super jet race car?"

"No. It's in the shop."

"Your rocket ship?"

"It's out of fuel."

"But... How will you get here? Your fire truck?!"

"The ladder is broken. I guess I'll have to walk."

"*Walk???* But by the time you get here, it'll be too late! What am I supposed to do?"

Brautigan Zeus rolled his eyes. "I'm not sure."

The boy was now crying and screaming, "Please *help me!* The fire... It's getting so *hot!!*"

"Ok, ok. Don't get all upset. I've got another vehicle. I'll come... *if*... you please stop all that fussing."

"Ok. I'm sorry."

And so Brautigan Zeus got out of bed and placed his propeller hat upon his head and at the speed of light, flew to the boy just in time, lassoed him up and brought him back to his mother. "There, are you happy?" he asked the boy.

"Yes!!! Thank you for the rescue, Brautigan Zeus! You're my hero!"

"You're welcome. Now, *I'm* going back to bed, so please don't get into any more monkey business."

"Ok," the boy yelled.

And Brautigan Zeus propelled back up into the sky and then back into his bed.

The End.

Was Angry Pirate

Hi, this is a nice ship, can I come aboard?
My first name is *Angry* and my last name is *Pirate!!!!!*
Oh, hello! Nice to meet you, Angry Pirate!
No, it's not. I told you my name to let you know I'm not in the mood for friends. That means, don't ever talk to me again, ok Matey?
Do you have any toys on your ship?
Arrrrg. Do you have glue in your ears? Didn't I just say *no talking*?
I just really want to know if you have any toys.
One more sound out of your smacker and I'll have you walk the plank! *Do you hear me?*
What are you so angry about?
I'm warning you, Matey! My name is Angry Pirate and that's all you need to know!
I bet I know what happened.
I bet you don't.
I bet someone took your toy.
What... did... you just say to me???
I said... I bet someone took your toy and that's why you're so angry. But I have toys, and I'll share them with you if you let me!
Did you just say you'll share your toys... with *me?* You would do that, Matey?
Why not?
I've been waiting 45 years for someone to share their toys with me...
That's a long time.
Come on in, Matey. But watch your step on this plank, there's alligators down there!!
Wow, you don't seem so angry anymore.
Ha! You know, you're right, Matey! I think I'm going to change my first name to Was!
Was Angry Pirate?
That's right!
Well, it's nice to meet you, Was.
You too, Matey!

Advice

Have you ever yawned in a windstorm without covering your mouth?
Don't do it. I'll tell you why.
My friend got a branch stuck in his mouth.
And his mother still can't get it out.

The End.

The Biggest Beach Towel

I know a boy named Mahabba Mahabba Mahabba Mahabba Mahabba Mahabba. And one day, he and his mama went to the beach and sat next to another mama and her boy. And Mahabba Mahabba Mahabba Mahabba Mahabba Mahabba noticed that the boy's towel had some letters on it. And so he asked the boy, "Excuse me, but what does your towel say?" And the boy said, "It spells my name. Max." And Mahabba Mahabba Mahabba Mahabba Mahabba Mahabba couldn't believe it. "Wow," he said. "I didn't know towels could say your name on them!" So he asked his mama, "Mama, can I have a towel that says *my* name on it?" And because his mama always gave him everything he wanted, she said, "Why of course you can!"

And so later that day, his mama called the personalized towel factory and ordered her son a towel. "Wow, that's a mouthful," the man told her. "Give us a couple months."

And a couple months later, a giant box was waiting for him on his stoop.

Mahabba Mahabba Mahabba Mahabba Mahabba Mahabba was so excited. He and his mama took the towel right to the beach. And as soon as he got there, he ran over to Max and waited for his mama who was lagging a bit behind because she needed a hand truck to carry the thing.

And after they unfurled this gigantic towel, every child at the beach ran over because they'd never seen such a giant towel. In fact, it was so big that every boy and girl at the entire beach could play on it. And so they did. And everyone had the best day they ever had.

The End.

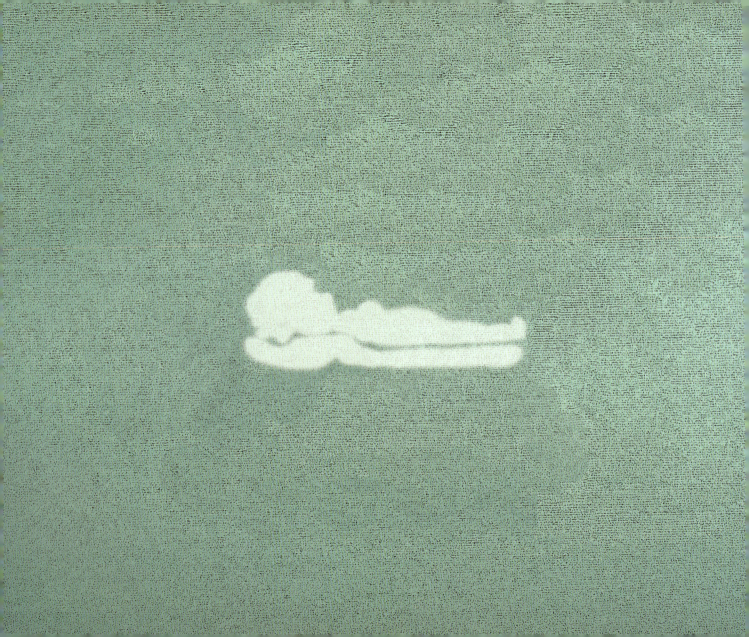

A Story Told By Clouds

    Once there was a scared little girl who was running from a bad guy and she turned into a fish so she could swim away faster and then she turned into a crown that had no head to sit upon and a dragon floated by and wanted to wear the crown but the crown said, "Sorry, too big for your head," and the crown turned into a bat and flew away towards a mouth with a long pony tail that was hungry as a fox, but the mouth was too far away to chomp anything so his chompers left his face and chomped a bit more before turning into the little girl again, except she was an old woman now, and she was so tired, so she found a fluffy pillow and went to sleep.

Show and Tell

Once there was a land where everyone wanted to show and tell.
Only there was no one left to notice.
The End.

Imaginary Friends

I have something I need to talk with you about.
What is it?
My mother told me you're just my imaginary friend.
Hm. That's interesting. Because my mother said the same thing about you. She says you're not real.
Could this just be a dream?
It could be. But how can we figure out which one of us is real, and which one of us is only a dream?
How about we pinch each other and see who feels it!
Ok.
Ow!
Ow!
Interesting.
Interesting indeed.
Well, maybe both our mothers are right.
Well, either way, I'm glad we're in the same dream.
Me, too. There's no one else's I'd rather be in!

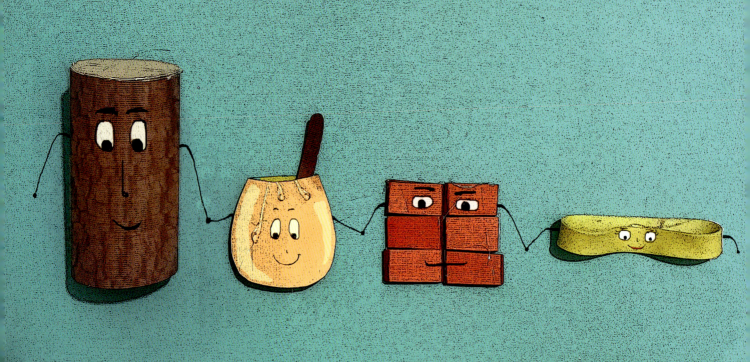

Enough Space for Everyone

I know we all have the same feelings and the same blood and tears and all that. But what you might not know is that underneath all that stuff, everyone's made of something different.

I'm made of honey, for instance. This means I flow without much effort. I make what's already there a little more special. But sometimes it's hard to clean up after me. My dad is a wood person. He kind of stays still a lot. But I can always count on him to be there. My mom is made of rubber. She bends easily, but if you stretch her too far she *will* snap and that's not so fun to be around. I have an aunt who's made of sugar. And sometimes, she's so sweet she can make you a little sick to your stomach. She's really nice, though, on special occasions.

And I know this big kid at school who's made of brick. And he *will not* budge, even if you ask nicely. And if you try to get him out of your way, forget it, you're likely to get hurt.

The other day I asked my teacher if she could please teach this kid how to be a little more flexible, but she said even brick people have a purpose. And so she gave him a job. Now he's the class supporter. Whenever anything falls apart, we call him over and he helps get things back to the way they're meant to be. He's happy. We're happy.

Like my teacher says, there's no use trying to turn anyone into something they're not. There's enough space in this world for everyone to be what they're made of, so long as they find a nice enough way to be useful.

The Contest

    Once I was eating french fries with my best friend and I was jealous that she had more than me. So I said, "Hey, let's have a contest to see who can eat their french fries the fastest!" And so she started gobbling them all up and guess what I did? I didn't eat a single one. I just sat there and watched till she had none. Then she looked at me and said, "I won, *I won!*" And I said, "Yes you did. But now you have no french fries." I then started eating mine with this horrible smile on my face. And that's when she started crying.

    "You're so mean!" she said.

    And when I realized she was right, the french fries suddenly tasted terrible. And then I started to cry, too.

    I knew there were only two things I could do: I could point off in the distance and shout, *"Look! An eagle!"* and run away when she wasn't looking, or I could say I'm sorry. I opted for saying sorry and I also gave her half my french fries. And not only did they taste yummy again, I realized that life is a lot happier when everyone gets to have what they want together.

                                             The End.

The Hippo Who Wanted A Story

Once there was a hippo who lived in a children's book and he realized one day that he wanted to hear a story about the little boy who was always reading about him. And so he asked the child if this would be ok. And the child said, "Sure," and started telling the hippo about how he woke up that morning and brushed his teeth. And the hippo said, "You brush your teeth?" And the child said, "Of course I do." And then the child said, "Do you want hear a story about me or do you want to ask a lot of questions?" And the hippo said, "Sorry, I'll listen to the story."

So the hippo listened from his swamp which was on the last page of his book as the boy went on and on. And he was right at the part about how he'd built a lego garage but shouldn't have built it naked because he sat on a lego and it really hurt, when his mother interrupted and told him it was time for bed.

His mother then rather abruptly closed the book and the hippo didn't even get to hear the rest of the boy's story. And from his bed, the little boy could still hear the hippo from inside the back cover of his book, begging from the bookshelf to know what happened next

The End.

The Longest Story in the World

Once upon a time there was a really looooooooooooooooooooooooooooooooooooooooooooooooooooooooooooooooooooooooooooooooooooooooooooooooooooooooooooooooooooooooooooooooooooooooooooooooooooooooooooooooooong story. But no one had enough breath to finish it.

The End.

Climbing the Titan Tree

My mommy told me NOT to climb the Titan Tree. If you have never heard of the Titan Tree, I'm going to tell you what it is. It's the biggest tree in the known universe. It stretches from Planet Earth all the way up to Titan. And it has a red caution ribbon around it with signs all over that say *DO NOT ENTER! DANGER!* But I really needed to climb the Titan Tree. Sometimes I'm in control of my brain and other times, I am not. This was one of those times I was not.

So I started to climb the tree. I passed squirrels and bird nests and then my head went through a cloud and almost knocked into a star. Then, I was too high for my own good and I started to cry. I could see the earth. I could see the blue and the green but I could not see my house or my mommy and this made me the most sad and the most scared I'd ever been.

Thank goodness my phone had a signal. So I called my mother and she was more than stern when I told her where I was. I have never heard my mother so upset. In fact she was so angry that her legs started to shake and grow bark. Right there on the sidewalk they turned into tree trunks that grew bigger and bigger while she was roaring into the phone about how angry she was. And in a matter of minutes, she and I were face to face at the tippy top of the Titan Tree.

Her face was made of birch and her arms were the longest branches and her mouth was so scary I hid behind her leaves. And then she grabbed me. I didn't know what she was going to do. Thank goodness she hugged me. Hugged me so close to her chest I could barely breath. I was crying, "I'm sorry, Mommy, I shouldn't have climbed the Titan Tree." And she was crying too. "I love you so much, but when are you going to start listening to me? *When?*" "Right now," I said. "Like the last right now?" "No," I said, "Like this new right now." And I hugged her back as tight as I could and we started shrinking down down down through outer space till we were back on the sidewalk again, like regular people.

And then my mommy took a deep breath. "How about we get some ice cream?" she said. And I said, "That sounds nice, Mommy." And so we did. And we had a nice rest of the day.

The End.

Stop Sign

One day, a little boy found out that grown-ups didn't know how to listen to anything except stop signs, so he decided to paste what he had to say to the one at the end of his street. And some of the grown-ups actually listened. At least until it was time for them to vroom again.

The End.

The Greatest Show

Have you ever seen a clown riding a unicycle into the woods? I never did. Until today. And I was curious. So I followed him, at a safe distance. And I watched him stop at a clearing and take out all his clown gear: his juggling balls, his rabbit in a hat, his cards.

His audience arrived moments later. About 12 or 13 forest animals who gathered around to watch. And just like that, his act began. Right in the sparkly snow. And this clown gave everything he had. What a show! The animals didn't clap or laugh, but they didn't run away either.

And when his show was over, he smiled and bowed and hopped back onto his unicycle and rode it back out to the street.

The End.

An Eye for an Eye

If we ever get mad at each other,
I'll give you my eye and you give me yours.
Just till we see where we're coming from.

The Boy Who Swallowed A Seed

Once there was a boy who swallowed a seed. He wanted it to grow so he opened his mouth as wide as he could, craned his neck toward the sun, and waited for its rays to reach deep inside. He stayed this way through rain and snow and more rain and more snow.

Then one warm day he felt a tickle in his belly. Day by day, the tickle grew. Until finally out of his mouth came the first branch, followed by the first blossom and first fruit. He was so proud, and all the people were in awe. They wanted his fruit and the boy gave it freely. And every time he gave more, he grew more.

Then one day he decided it was time to close his mouth. But when he tried, he couldn't. The tree had taken over. Its roots had become his roots. Its branches, his branches. Its blossoms, his blossoms. And though at first this made him nervous, when he thought it through, he realized there was nothing more he wanted than the sun and rain and nothing more he'd rather give than all his fruit.

My Shadow

If you see me out and about, please be careful not to step on my shadow because it gets hurt easily and it's very tired of being walked over again and again.

The End.

The Highest Leaves

There was a giraffe who wanted some leaves he couldn't reach. Mind you, there were tons of other leaves he *could* reach. He was a giraffe, after all. But he couldn't stop thinking about these out-of-reach leaves. And he also couldn't stop talking about these out-of-reach leaves with every giraffe who would stick around to listen.

"Would you stop thinking about leaves you can't reach and be happy with these leaves right here?"

"What makes you think they're any better anyhow?"

"You're going to drive yourself and the rest of us nuts!"

But the giraffe couldn't control his brain so he made himself some stilts.

When he walked into the village with them on, everyone was terrified. But the extra-tall giraffe didn't care. He was too busy making a beeline to his tree. Finally he was eye-to-eye with those higher leaves. The giraffe was drooling. "Ok," he said. "Here I go." And he started chomping. After chomping for some time, something made him look down. And when he did, he saw all his giraffe friends staring up with such longing. They looked so small down there. And they weren't even chomping like they always chomped. They were too busy wondering if maybe they were missing out. That maybe those higher leaves were better after all.

The giraffe on stilts began to feel sad. Not only because the higher leaves really weren't better than the others. And not only because his back was aching from being on stilts. But because he missed his friends. And so he tossed a bunch of leaves down to prove they tasted just the same, took off his stilts, and began chomping the leaves he could reach without suffering. And he never wore his stilts again.

The End.

Has Anybody Seen My Stick?

Has anyone seen my stick?
I lost it in these woods.
It's thin and brown and maybe long...
It's one of a kind...
And I'm not leaving till I find it.

He Carried His Love on the Top of His Head

There was once a man who carried his love on the top his head. For the most part there were no problems. But sometimes if he wasn't paying attention, his love would fall off. And in those moments, when his love was lost, he was not so nice to be around. He'd get down on his hands and knees and yell at everyone, "Get out of my way! I'm looking for my love! Don't touch it or I'll *destroy you!*" But as soon as he found it, and placed it back on the top of his head, he was himself again.

Feed It to the Worms

If you ever get scared, or mean, and you wonder if maybe you're not
such a good or brave kid after all... I'll tell you what you do:
Take those feelings and feed 'em to the wormies.
"Did you say wormies?"
Yes, I did. Did you know, no matter where you are,
underneath you, there's a world of wormies?
Even if you're on the top of a skyscraper or on an airplane-
way down under the ground, the wormies are there. And they're hungry.
And you know what they like to eat best? All your bad feelings.
Tastes just like pizza to them. Yup. Even the ones that make you want to
bite your mom, or make you wanna throw your toys,
or make you wake up crying in the middle of the night.
Just gather them all up and toss 'em all down.
The wormies'll thank you.
They thank me all the time!

The Boy with the Heavy Suitcase

Once there was a little boy who carried a suitcase wherever he went. He never let it go, even though it was cumbersome and prevented him from having much fun. One day his friend got fed up. She had tried to climb a tree with the boy, but his suitcase slipped off a branch and hit her in the head. "Why are you always carrying that thing??" she asked. "It makes playing with you so difficult! It's always in the way!"

"I have to carry it," he said, annoyed.

"Why? What's inside?"

The boy really didn't want to tell, but the girl was his best friend, after all. "Fine," he said. "It's something mean someone said to me a long time ago."

"But why do you carry it wherever you go?"

"Because I don't want anyone else to find out."

The girl finally convinced him to open it up. And when he did, she sighed. "You've gotta be kidding me," she said. "This has nothing to do with you! You've been carrying around someone else's stuff! You have to give it back!" So the boy packed up what he'd been carrying for so long and shipped it back to its owner with a note:

> *I've been carrying around something you gave me a long time ago, and I realize I don't want it anymore. So I'm sending it back.*

Without his suitcase, the boy felt better than ever. He could climb anywhere and play anything and no one got hurt or confused by his big load.

Then, a few weeks later, he received a letter:

> *Thank you for sending back what I gave you so long ago. I had forgotten about it. I feel badly you carried it for so long. It wasn't really supposed to be for you. Someone else had given it to me and I didn't know what else to do, so I gave it to you. I have since returned it to its proper owner. Please accept an apology instead. I hope that will be easier to carry.*

So the boy accepted the apology, which he didn't need a suitcase for, and he and his friend enjoyed the rest of their day.

The End

The Danger Dangerouses

The Danger Dangerouses are so dangerous, they ride on top of cars
instead of driving them inside.
They're so dangerous, they sail their boats over waterfalls.
Their babies lean out of screen windows even though there's a sign saying not to.
There's no way to stop them.
Except that they're not real.
But they're so dangerous, they want to be.

A Case of the What Ifs

Mama, I don't think we should leave the nest today.
Why not?
Well, what if I fly to the bird feeder and the cat eats me? Or what if the cat eats you?
Oh my goodness! Sounds like you woke up with A Case of The What Ifs!
The What Ifs?
It's when the mind starts thinking of everything that could possibly go wrong.
Oh no... Is there any cure?
Yes in fact, there is! For every What If, all you have to do is look around and notice What's Actually Happening Right Now.
What do you mean?
Well, can you tell me something that's actually happening right now?
I see the sun shining.
Yes.... And how does it make you feel?
Warm!
Anything else?
I feel the wind blowing my feathers! I never noticed that before!
Very good!
And I see you, Mama! And that makes my heart feel happy.
Aw, my heart feels happy to see you, too! There are always bad things that *could* happen. But if you spend all your time worrying, you'll miss out on all the wonderful things that are actually happening right now!
And if that mangy cat does come around, I'll already be paying attention to what's happening, so we can just fly right back up to our nest!
Good thinking!
Thank you, Mama.
Of course, my Little Bird. Now let's go get some breakfast!

Hide and Seek

Once I played hide and seek but instead of hiding behind the curtain like
I usually do, I flew to another country.
And it took the police to find me.
I have never played that game again.
And I am no longer friends with the person I played it with.

The End.

The Girl Who Wanted To Be Someone Else

Janie Blaine wanted to be someone else. Not just any someone else. She wanted to be like the new girl at school. The new girl at school could do a cartwheel on the balance beam. Everyone was so impressed. She even got a standing ovation. Janie wanted a standing ovation, too. But when she tried the cartwheel, she almost broke her leg.

The new girl also had freckles, so Janie figured freckles would be a safer bet. So she dotted her cheeks with a brown marker, but on the way to school, her mother wiped them off. "The new girl at school has freckles," Janie explained. "Well, that's fine for the new girl at school. Your skin is perfect just the way it is."

The new girl at school also had bangs, so Janie thought this might be the answer. So she found some scissors and was about to use them when her mother walked in. "What in the world are you doing *now!?*"

"Bangs, Mommy. The new girl at school has them."

"But your hair is perfect just the way it is!"

Then, Janie stared to cry.

"Why in the world do you keep trying to be like somebody else?" her mother asked.

Janie shrugged.

"Do you know what would happen if you really did turn into someone else?"

"No."

"No one would get to be you! And the world would be deprived of the most special person I know."

Janie smiled, and from that moment on, she decided to be herself.

Peck, Peck, Peck

Once upon a time, I gave a woodpecker a sandwich. He couldn't believe it. *"All our lives,"* he cried. "Pecking away at trees... giving ourselves headaches... and we could have been eating sandwiches!?"

I felt so terrible, I made him some to bring back to his family.

His family had a similar reaction. But once they calmed down, they were glad to have the sandwiches.

And ever since, the forest has been much more peaceful. Though I wish they could figure out how to make the sandwiches by themselves.

The End

The Land of the Grown-Ups that Never Grew Up

I went on a field trip to this land where grown-ups never grow up. They still look big and hairy and they run banks and drive cars and make phone calls but trust me, nothing else about them is normal.

As soon as we got there, 10 or 15 of them surrounded the bus. They were climbing through the windows and shouting, "*What did you bring us??!!*" My teacher smiled politely and told our class to get in a single file line and we headed into town.

We visited the gift shop and the owner was having a meltdown at the counter. He was pulling his hair and crying because we were touching his merchandise. "*Don't touch that candy,*" he kept yelling.

"But I was going to buy some," I said.

"It's *mine*," he cried. "NOT YOURS!"

"But... I thought this was a store!"

He stomped his foot and another grown-up ran out full force and I thought she was going to straighten this whole mess out but instead she tried to bite me. "*Stay away from my friend or I'll cage you!*"

"But... I was just trying to buy some candy!"

"*Stop talking!*" she screamed, and then she put her fingers deep in her ears.

That's when my teacher whispered to me, "Don't forget, sweetie. We're in the Land where grown-ups never grow up."

"Oh yeah!" I said, and I laughed.

When it was time to head back to school, a bunch of the grown-ups wouldn't get off our bus. A few of them were pretending to steer the wheel and one was smearing the bus driver's face with what might have been paint.

My teacher didn't know what to do.

Thankfully, I had some pennies in my pocket so I said, "Hey guys! Who wants a penny?" They all raised their hands and shouted, "*Me me me!*" And so I tossed the pennies out the bus door and as soon as the grown-ups ran for them, our bus driver stepped on it and we zoomed home.

"I don't think I ever want to go there again," I said to my friend.

"That makes two of us," he said.

The End.

Enough Love for Everyone

I don't love myself.
Why not?
I only love you.
Well, what if I love you with the love you give me? Then you'll get to feel what your own love feels like!
Ok.
Do you feel your love yet?
Yes! Thank you. But what about you? Now you don't feel loved...
Yes I do! There must have been extra.
But how do we know whose love we're feeling?
I don't know. Maybe it doesn't matter.
Maybe you're right.

A Planet Called Earth

Once there was a planet where a lot of people lived.
Sometimes they made a mess.
And sometimes they made a bigger mess.

The End.

Box of Bad Guys

What would you do if you had a box of bad guys? I'll tell you what I did. Nothing. Well, I kept it under my bed. And I looked at it at least once a day. And I wanted to open it, but I was afraid of what I'd see. I was afraid of all those bad guys and I was afraid of what they'd do to not only me but to the people I loved.

And I didn't want to tell anyone about it because I didn't want anyone else to open it up and get hurt either. You never know what a bunch of bad guys are capable of. Especially a bunch of bad guys who've been shut in a box for a really long time.

So I kept it under the bed. And there it stayed, for a lot of years. Until I had a boy of my own, who found the box one day. And he brought it to me because it said *Do Not Open*, and he said, "Daddy, what's in the box?" And then he said, "Daddy, why's your face so red?"

I could hardly talk. The last thing in the world I wanted was for my boy to open this box and see a bunch of bad guys flying out and doing whatever horrible thing they were gonna do. So I yelled, *"Don't open it!!!"* But it was too late. He opened the box. And there, before our very eyes, were a bunch of bad guys. Except they were really old. And they were just lying in the box on their beds with these long white beards and bald heads. And I said, "Wait a minute. Are you guys bad guys or what? All these years, I was afraid to open this box because there were bad guys in here!" And one of the guys yawned and said, "Yeah, Sonny, I know. We *were* bad guys. Really, really bad guys. But now we're just old and tired guys. All our bad ideas and bad feelings have worn away. And now all we want to do is rest and think about things. So can you please close the box back up?" And me and my boy, we looked at these old guys and nodded yes. "Of course. We'll close it back up."

"Great," they all said. "And put us where we won't be disturbed again."
"Alright."
And so we put the box in the basement. And no one ever opened it up again.
The End.

Heart Phone

    A little boy used to talk to his grand-mère on the phone everyday. She used to call him Mr. Octopus and he called her Mrs. Octopus. But then one day she got sick and went to heaven. They have phones in heaven. But you have to answer them in your heart, and it takes a little practice to get good reception. But once he figured it out, the little boy could call whenever he wanted and his grand-mère was always right there.

The Joke With No Punchline

A mosquito landed on my arm and I was about to swat it, when it looked at me with its big buggy eyes and said, "Hold on! I've got jokes!"
"Come on," I said.
"Please! *I'm begging!*"
"It's rude to beg."
"I've got family at home!"
"You do?"
"15,000 nieces and nephews!"
"Wow."
"Come on, lemme tell you a joke. At least we can have a good laugh."
"I was already gonna let you go."
"How 'bout one for the road?"
"Fine. Go ahead."
"Ok. Here I go... A mosquito... *got a mosquito bite!!!!!!*" The mosquito roared with laughter.
"That's it?" I asked.
"Wait," he said, trying to catch his breath. "I've got another one: An apple... *ate a banana!!*"
This time, the mosquito laughed so hard he got the hiccups.
"Hold on," I said. "I don't even know why you're laughing. Your jokes have no punchlines."
"*Punchlines?* Punchlines are for other people! I tell these jokes for myself."
I sighed. This mosquito was really exhausting me. "I should have just let you bite me," I said.
"Come on. Try a joke. I guarantee you'll laugh."
"You want me to tell my own joke so that *I* can laugh?"
"That's right."
"Fine, fine... Oh, forget it. I can't think of anything."
"Yes you can. Get out of your own way!"
"Ok, fine," I said. "Here I go: There's a... *pig lost in my brain!!*"
And the mosquito was right. Sure enough, I couldn't stop laughing. Over and over I repeated my joke till tears were streaming down my face. The mosquito was so happy for me. "Tell another one!" he said.
"Ok, ok," I said, trying to catch my breath. "My mother's nose... *is a spoon!!*"
This time, I almost had an accident in my pants, I was laughing so hard. In fact I was laughing so hard I didn't even notice that the mosquito had flown away, and that my mother was now standing in front of me with her hands on her hips. "My nose is a spoon, huh?"
"Sorry, Mommy," I said. "It's a joke."
"I see."
"A mosquito taught me how to tell jokes!"
"Oh, really. A mosquito? Well, it's a good thing I came out with some bug spray."
And she sprayed me silly.

The End.

The Mouse Who Got His Own House

There was a mouse in someone's house and he poopooed everywhere.
It was not the usual sort of mouse poo, though.
This mouse poopooed money.
In fact, he poopooed so much money, that the people collected it and bought the mouse a house of his own.

The End.

The Elephant and the Glass House

Once there was an elephant who really wanted, more than anything in the world, to live in a glass house. Everyone in town told him it was a bad idea. But the elephant didn't think it was a bad idea at all. He could just picture himself lying in his bed at night, looking up through the ceiling at the moon.

The neighbors shook their heads out their windows watching the elephant's building crew. And a year later, it was finally done.

Just as everyone predicted, on moving-in day, the elephant didn't make it past the front stoop. The glass stairs smashed and the elephant sprained his trunk. All the neighbors came running out of their houses to help him up.

"Go ahead," the elephant cried. "You can say it. You told me so. Go ahead. I deserve it."

But at that moment, his neighbors said nothing. Even Mr. Pigeon, who'd been practicing in the mirror for months exactly how he'd tell the elephant he told him so, said nothing.

His neighbors said nothing because at that moment, they could see how badly the elephant had wanted to live in his glass house and how sad he was that he'd never ever get to.

After a minute or two of silence, Mrs. Beaver asked a question. "Is there anything else you'd want almost as much as a glass house? Maybe we can help you get it."

All the neighbors thought this was a great idea. Even Mr. Pigeon. And the elephant thought about it for a minute or so and said, "Well, the only other thing I've ever really wanted, besides my glass house, is for all of you to want to be my friends." And this time, he got what he wanted.

The End.

Snail Race

You know what's the worst job in the whole world?
Worse than cleaning your room?
Being a judge at the snail races.
I've been sitting here 14 days.

The Ant in the Sandwich Shop

There was this ant. And he was in line to get a sandwich. It was a big line, but the ant had a big voice. So when the kid behind him tried to squash him, he yelled, "Hey kid, can't an ant get a sandwich around here without being harassed?"

At the last minute, he wound up ordering a salad because he figured it'd be healthier. And just as he was pouring on the vinaigrette, a lady passing by screamed, "There's an *ant* in that *salad!!!*" And the ant yelled at her. He said, "Lady, why are you screaming at me? You think just because you've seen a few ants in your life that we're all the same? Come on. Get with a new program."

And the lady realized the ant was a customer just like she was. And she said she was sorry. And she promised never to squash another ant ever again. And the ant finished his meal in peace.

The End

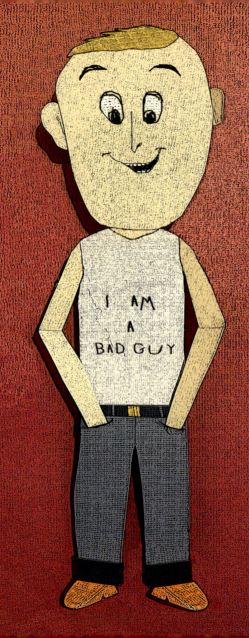

Raise Your Hand If You're A Bad Guy

"Attention People of Planet Earth!!! I've started a new company! It's a shirt company for bad guys! It says, 'I am a bad guy' on it so everyone knows which people are the bad guys! So if you're a bad guy, please raise your hand, because I've got a shirt for you! Thanks!!!"

The Scary Ghost

There was once a ghost that wouldn't stop scaring a little boy. Everywhere the boy went, the ghost followed yelling, "Ooooooooohhhh! Ooooooooohhhh! *Ooooooooohh!*" At first the little boy was scared. Really scared. But after awhile, he got pretty tired of seeing this glowing white bully all the time. So one day, he said to the ghost, "Ok, enough is enough. Take off your smock and show yourself!!"

The ghost was startled. "Ooooh," he yelled, trying to frighten the boy away. But the little boy stood his ground. "I said, show yourself! *Right now!!!*" And so the ghost took off his white scary ghost garb and the boy stared with wide eyes at what was underneath. Which was Nothing. Not a single solitary thing. "So, let me get this straight," said the boy. "Without all that malarkey, you're just *Nothing?*"

The ghost nodded his invisible head.

"I can't see you, remember? So *speak up!*"

"Yes, yes, it's true," said the ghost. "Without my ghost garb, I'm... Nothing!"

Then the ghost started to cry.

"You're sure upset," said the little boy. "It's ok to be upset sometimes. So I'm gonna give you 15 more seconds to get it all out and then we're gonna buck up and fix this together, all right?"

The ghost nodded his invisible head again and in 15 seconds, he stopped crying.

By this time, the boy had already gone to his closet and come back with a new outfit for the ghost. "Here," he said, dangling the shirt and pants. "See if these fit."

In a few minutes, the ghost was all dressed. He still didn't have a body, but at least he was a little more recognizable. "Thanks," the ghost said.

"Now," said the boy. "You need a face." So the boy went to his art supply bin and grabbed some paint. "You want to be happy?" "Yeah," said the ghost.

And so the boy gave him a big smile. And then some arms and legs.

"Now you just need a name. How about Gary?"

"I like Gary," said the ghost.

"Looks like you're feeling better already," said the boy.

"Yeah. A lot better," said the ghost.

"Good. Now let's go outside and play."

And they did.

The End.

The Day The Mourning Doves Almost Got Divorced

I woke up to a couple mourning doves fighting in my garden. They were yelling at each other nonstop to the point where I had to go outside and say, "Guys, *what* is going on?"

They both folded their wings and looked at the sky instead of each other and tapped their feet. And I said, "Hey, don't you guys mate for life?" And they both shrugged.

"Come on, don't tell me you're gonna be the first mourning doves to get divorced?!" They shrugged again. "You're gonna ruin your family's tradition? Over what? What could be the big deal?"

And they both blurted out together, "She doesn't listen to me!" "He doesn't listen to me!" And then they both said, "*See?*"

"Oh boy," I said. "I know what the problem is. Neither of you are wearing thinking caps."

"*What??*" they both yelled. "Birds don't wear *thinking caps!*"

"Hold on," I said. And I went to my craft bin and made a couple really tiny caps and placed them on their tiny heads. And after a minute, they both smiled.

"You look funny," the one said to the other. "Oh yeah?" she laughed. "You look pretty funny yourself." And then they both started laughing.

"Now," I said. "Whenever you get mad at each other, just put on your thinking caps and look at each other till you find something funny enough to laugh about. Ok??"

And every morning since, I get woken up by these guys laughing their beaks off.

The End.

How to Fill an Empty Heart

My heart is empty.
I have some loose change... Wanna stack some up in there?
Nah.
I could help you rent it out to someone else, so you could buy a full one with the proceeds...
Nah.
How about get some topsoil and plant flowers in it? That might look pretty.
No thanks.
You could hire a detective to find what used to be there...
No.
Maybe you could just pretend it isn't empty.
I don't think so.
You could eat a lot of cookies and ask your belly to share...?
Nah.
You could steal a full heart and try to shove it in yours.
No.
Or you could cry and hope someone might hear you and help...
I guess.
Or... I suppose you could ask someone you love if they could please fill it back up.
I think I'll try that last one. Could you please fill my empty heart?
Sure! How 'bout a hug?
Much better. Thank you!
You're welcome!

A Story In Threes

Once once once upon upon upon a time time time, there was was was a little little little boy boy boy. He he he had had had three three three heads heads heads and three three three thoughts thoughts thoughts so one one one day day day he went went went online line line and ordered ordered ordered a nother nother nother head head head and then he had four four four four.
The the the the end end end end.

Table of Contents

My Elevator - 5
The Boy Who Befored His Daddy's Ear - 7
The Unanswerable Question - 9
The Kind King - 11
Too Many Toys - 13
Mean Red - 15
The Girl With Seven Ears - 17
The Three-Legged Cow - 19
Thinking Cap - 21
The Day Everyone's Feelings Got Hurt - 23
The Big Misunderstanding - 25
The Boy Who Was Afraid To Cry - 27
The Little Boy and His Friend - 29
The Girl Who Wouldn't Take A Bath - 31
Ripping Service - 33
The Reluctant Rescuer - 35
Was Angry Pirate - 37
Advice - 39
The Biggest Beach Towel - 41
A Story Told by Clouds - 43
Show and Tell - 45
Imaginary Friends - 47
Enough Space For Everyone - 49
The Contest - 51
The Hippo Who Wanted A Story - 53
The Longest Story in the World - 55
Climbing the Titan Tree - 57
Stop Sign - 59
The Greatest Show - 61

An Eye for an Eye - 63
The Boy Who Swallowed a Seed - 65
My Shadow - 67
The Highest Leaves - 69
Has Anybody Seen My Stick? - 71
He Carried His Love on the Top of His Head - 73
Feed It to the Worms - 75
The Boy with the Heavy Suitcase - 77
The Danger Dangerouses - 79
A Case of the What Ifs - 81
Hide and Seek - 83
The Girl Who Wanted to be Someone Else - 85
Peck, Peck, Peck - 87
The Land of the Grown-Ups that Never Grew Up - 89
A Planet Called Earth - 91
How to Fill an Empty Heart - 93
Box of Bad Guys - 95
Heart Phone - 97
The Joke with No Punchline - 99
The Mouse Who Got His Own House - 101
The Elephant and the Glass House - 103
Snail Race - 105
The Ant in the Sandwich Shop - 107
Raise Your Hand If You're A Bad Guy - 109
The Scary Ghost - 111
The Day The Mourning Doves Almost Got Divorced - 113
Enough Love for Everyone - 115
A Story In Threes - 117
The End.

Acknowledgments

A special thank you to my son Brautigan, who is the inspiration for all these stories. To my husband Chris, my endless source of encouragement. And to the spirit of my mother, who is always here on my heart phone, helping me edit.